Introduction by W. Terrence Gordon

In this introduction to the first reprinting of *The Bias of Communication* by Harold A. Innis, Toronto: University of Toronto Press, 1964 (first edition, 1951), pages vii-xvi, McLuhan is, in many respects, describing himself and his own manner of working. This does not prevent him from being sharply critical of Innis, upon whom he builds. McLuhan's insight that Innis had been misunderstood because he worked with the causality principle did not prevent him from working with the same principle himself. McLuhan enlightened Innis about the esthetic discoveries of the French Symbolists and how their legacy had been nurtured in English literature by Joyce, Eliot, Pound, Lewis, and Yeats. In spite of Innis's failure to make the distinction so critical to McLuhan himself, between mechanical and electronic technologies, he acknowledged Innis's genius and the debt he owed Innis for opening the way to an epistemology of experience. Pivotal ideas in *The Gutenberg Galaxy* and *Understanding Media* and even later in McLuhan's writings would be drawn from Innis. So, when McLuhan moved, relatively late in his career, to a figure-ground approach to media analysis, he acknowledged that Innis had been there before him. McLuhan gave Innis the credit for the basis of his own work on the economy of the sensorium (the relationship among the five physical senses), and Innis's phrase "the nemesis of creativity" made its way into *Understanding Media* as a chapter heading. — WTG

Introduction by Marshall McLuhan to:

The Bias of Communication

[Harold A. Innis, first edition, 1951]

For anyone acquainted with poetry since Baudelaire and with painting since Cézanne, the later world of Harold A. Innis is quite readily intelligible. He brought their kinds of contemporary awareness of the electric age to organize the data of the historian and the social scientist. Without having studied modern art and poetry, he yet discovered how to arrange his insights in patterns that nearly resemble the art forms of our time. Innis presents his insights in a mosaic structure of seemingly unrelated and disproportioned sentences and aphorisms. Such is page 108, for example, with its scholarly footnote that will certainly bear looking into. Anybody who has looked up the reference material that Innis cites so frequently will be struck by the skill with which he has extracted exciting facts from dull expositions. He explored his source material with a "Geiger counter," as it were. In turn, he presents his finds in a pattern of insights that are not packaged for the consumer palate. He expects the reader to make discovery after discovery that he himself had missed. His view of the departmentalized specialisms of our Universities as ignoble monopolies of knowledge is expressed on page 194: "Finally we must keep in mind the limited role of Universities and recall the comment that 'the whole external history of science is a history of the resistance of academies and Universities to the progress of knowledge.' "

One can say of Innis what Bertrand Russell said of Einstein on the first page of his *A B C of Relativity* (1925): "Many of the new ideas can be expressed in non-mathematical language, but they are none the less difficult on that account. What is demanded is a change in our imaginative picture of the world." The "later Innis" who dominates *The Bias of Communication* had set out on a quest for the causes of change. The "early Innis" of *The Fur Trade in Canada* had conformed a good deal to the conventional patterns of merely reporting and narrating change. Only at the conclusion of *The Fur Trade in Canada* study did he venture to interlace or link complex events in a way that reveals the causal processes of change. His insight that the American Revolution was in large part due to a clash between the interests of the settlers on one hand, and the interests of the fur traders on the other, is the sort of vision that becomes typical of the later Innis. He changed his procedure from working with a "point of view" to that of the generating of insights by the method of "interface," as it is named in chemistry. "Interface" refers to the interaction of substances in a kind of mutual irritation. In art and poetry this is precisely the technique of "symbolism" (Greek, *symballein* — to throw together) with its paratactic procedure of juxtaposing without connectives. It is the natural form of conversation or dialogue rather than of written discourse. In writing, the tendency is to isolate an aspect of some matter and to direct steady attention upon that aspect. In dialogue there is an equally natural interplay of multiple aspects of any matter. This interplay of aspects can generate insights or discovery. By contrast, a point of view is merely a way of *looking at* something. But an insight is the sudden awareness of a complex process of interaction. An insight is a contact with the life of forms. Students of computer programming have had to learn how to approach all knowledge structurally. In order to transfer any kind of knowledge to tapes it is necessary to understand the form of that knowledge. This has led to the discovery of the basic difference between classified knowledge and pattern recognition. It is a helpful distinction to keep in mind when reading Innis since he is above all a recognizer of patterns. Dr. Kenneth Sayre explains the matter as follows in his *The Modelling of Mind* (University of Notre Dame Press, 1963, page 17): "Classification is a *process*, something which takes up one's time, which one might do reluctantly, unwillingly, or unenthusiastically, which can be done with more or less success, done very well or very poorly. Recognition, in sharp contrast, is not time-consuming. A person may spend a long while looking before recognition occurs, but when it occurs it is 'instantaneous.' When recognition occurs, it is not an act which would be said to be performed either reluctantly or enthusiastically, compliantly or under protest. Moreover, the notion of recognition being unsuccessful, or having been done very poorly, seems to make no sense at all."

In this book, Innis has much to say about the oral as opposed to the written methods of approaching the learning process. In the paper titled "A Critical Review," he explains: "My bias is with the oral tradition, particularly as reflected in Greek civilization, and with the necessity of recapturing something of its spirit." (page 190) E. A. Havelock, a former colleague of Innis, has recently devoted an entire study to the clash of the old oral and the new written culture of Greece. His *Preface to Plato* (Harvard, 1963) would have delighted Innis, and there are very many sentences in Innis which should become the subject of such full investigations.

I am pleased to think of my own book *The Gutenberg Galaxy* (University of Toronto Press, 1962) as a footnote to the observations of Innis on the subject of the psychic and social consequences, first of writing then of printing. Flattered by the attention that Innis had directed to some work of mine, I turned for the first time to his work. It was my good fortune to begin with the first essay in this book, "Minerva's Owl." How exciting it was to encounter a writer whose every phrase invited prolonged meditation and exploration: "Alexandria broke the link between science and philosophy. The library was an imperial instrument to offset the influence of Egyptian priesthood." (page 10)

Innis takes much time to read if he is read on his own terms. That he deserves to be read on his own terms becomes obvious as soon as that experiment is tried even once. So read, he takes time but he also saves time. Each sentence is a compressed monograph. He includes a small library on each page, and often incorporates a small library of references on the same page in addition. If the business of the teacher is to save the student's time, Innis is one of the greatest teachers on record. The two sentences just quoted imply and invite an awareness of the specific structural forms of science and philosophy as well as of the structural nature and functions of empires, libraries and priesthoods. Most writers are occupied in providing accounts of the contents of philosophy, science, libraries, empires and religions. Innis invites us instead to consider the formalities of power exerted by these structures in their mutual interaction. He approaches each of these forms of organized power as exercising a particular kind of force upon each of the other components in the complex. All of the components exist by virtue of processes going on within each and among them all. Just what "science" or "philosophy" was at this time will be manifested by what each does to the other in their encounter in the social and historic process. And so with the other components. They explain themselves by their behaviour in an historic action. Innis had hit upon the means of using history as the physicist uses the cloud chamber. By bouncing the unknown form against known forms, he discovered the nature of the new or little known form.

This use of history as a scientific laboratory, as a set of controlled conditions within which to study the life and nature of forms, is very far removed from the conventional narrative of a Toynbee. Toynbee is like the announcer of a sporting event. He tells a good deal about what is happening. His tone of earnest concern indicates to the reader or listener that the events have some significance. In the same situation Innis would have observed that the form of the sporting event was an interesting model of perception, giving us an immediate image of the motives and patterns of the society that had invented this corporate extension of itself.

He would then explain that his role of announcer, like that of the audience at the sporting event, was part of the structure of the game, having a distorting bias of perception and amplification that gave the game in question a great deal of political and commercial force.

As soon as the reader grasps that Innis is concerned with the unique power of each form to alter the action of other forms it encounters, he will be able to proceed as Innis did. He can begin to observe and estimate the action and counteraction of forms past and present. He will discover that Innis never repeats himself, but that he never ceases to test the action of oral forms of knowledge and social organization in different social contexts. Innis tests the oral form as it reacts in many different written cultures, just as he tests the effects of time-structured institutions in their varieties of contact with space-oriented societies.

It would be a mistake to suppose that Innis has garnered most of the available insights from any given historical test that he happens to run. In the same way, he is quite capable of inaccurate observation during the running of his tests of the interactions of social forms, though this in no way impairs the validity of his way of testing the structural properties of social forms. For example, he notes that: "The Greeks took over the alphabet and made it a flexible instrument suited to the demands of a flexible oral tradition by the creation of words." (page 7) The alphabet is a technology of visual fragmentation and specialism, and it led the Greeks quickly to the discovery of classifiable data. Havelock clarifies this at length in his *Preface to Plato*. As long as the oral culture was not overpowered by the technological extension of the visual power in the alphabet, there was a very rich cultural result from the interplay of the oral and written forms. The revival of oral culture in our own electric age now exists in a similar fecund relation with the still powerful written and visual culture. We are in our century "winding the tape backwards." The Greeks went from oral to written even as we are moving from written to oral. They "ended" in a desert of classified data even as we could "end" in a new tribal encyclopedia of auditory incantation.

Innis sometimes mistook the interplay of written and oral forms, ascribing to the written form itself what was a hybrid product of its interaction with oral culture: "The alphabet borrowed from the Phoenicians was given vowels and adapted to the demands of speech. The ear replaced the eye. With the spread of writing the oral tradition developed fresh powers of resistance evident in the flowering of Greek culture in the sixth and fifth centuries." (page 136) Had Innis made a more intense analysis of the visual modalities inherent in the phonetic alphabet, or a more thorough study of the dynamics of oral forms, he would have avoided some of these slips. But the method he discovered remains. He had discovered a means of using historical situations as a lab in which to test the character of technology in the shaping of cultures.

Innis taught us how to use the bias of culture and communication as an instrument of research. By directing attention to the bias or distorting power of the dominant imagery and technology of any culture, he showed us how to understand cultures. Many scholars had made us aware of the "difficulty of assessing the quality of a culture of which we are a part or of assessing the quality of a culture of which we are not a part." (page 132) Innis was perhaps the first to make of this vulnerable fact of all scholarly outlook the prime opportunity for research and discovery. Peter F. Drucker in *Managing for Results* (Harper & Row, 1964) has shown how in any human organization or situation 90% of the events are caused by 10%. Most human attention is allocated to the 90% area which is the area of problems. The 10% area is the area of irritation and also of opportunity. It was the genius of Harold Innis that he refused to be distracted by the 90% area of problems. He went straight to the 10% core of opportunity and sought insight into the causes that underlay the whole situation. For example, he writes: "We are perhaps too much a part of the civilization which followed the printing industry to be able to detect its characteristics. Education in the words of Laski became the art of teaching men to be deceived by the printed word." (page 139)

Once Innis had ascertained the dominant technology of a culture he could be sure that this was the cause and shaping force of the entire structure. He could also be sure that this dominant form and all its causal powers were necessarily masked from the attention of that culture by a psychic mechanism of "protective inhibition," as it were. At a stroke he had solved two major problems that are forever beyond the power of the "nose-counters" and of statistical researchers. First, he knew what the pattern of any culture had to be, both psychically and socially, as soon as he had identified its major technological achievements. Second, he knew exactly what the members of that culture would be ignorant of in their daily lives. What has been called "the nemesis of creativity" is precisely a blindness to the effects of one's most significant form of invention.

A good example of this technological blindness in Innis himself was his mistake in regarding radio and electric technology as a further extension of the patterns of mechanical technology: "The radio appealed to vast areas, overcame the division between classes in its escape from literacy, and favoured centralization and bureaucracy." (page 82) Again: "Competition from the new medium, the radio, involved an appeal to the ear rather than to the eye and consequently an emphasis on centralization." (page 188) This is an example of Innis failing to be true to his own method. After many historical demonstrations of the space-binding power of the eye and the time-binding power of the ear, Innis refrains from applying these structural principles to the action of radio. Suddenly, he shifts the ear world of radio into the visual orbit, attributing to radio all the centralizing powers of the eye and of visual culture. Here Innis was misled by the ordinary consensus of his time. Electric light and power, like all electric media, are profoundly decentralizing and separatist in their psychic and social consequences. Had he not been hypnotized by his respect for the pervasive conventional view on this question, Innis could have worked out the new electric pattern of culture quite easily.

What is rare in Innis occurs in his mention of the views of Wyndham Lewis: "Wyndham Lewis has argued that the fashionable mind is the time-denying mind." He is referring to *Time and Western Man*, which is devoted to a denunciation of the obsession with time as a religious mystique in the work of Bergson, Alexander, Whitehead and others. Because of his own deep concern with the values of tradition and temporal continuity, Innis has managed to misread Wyndham Lewis radically. Earlier in the same essay, "A Plea for Time," he raises an issue that may bear on the occasional miscarriage of his own structural method of analysis. Speaking of the unfortunate effects of the extreme development of print on our twentieth century culture, he observes: "Communication based on the eye in terms of printing and photography had developed a monopoly which threatened to destroy Western civilization first in war and then in peace." (page 80) Innis did not like monopolies in any form. He saw that they bred violent reactions: "The disastrous effect of the monopoly of communication based on the eye hastened the development of a competitive type of communication based on the ear, in the radio and in the linking of sound to the cinema and to television. Printed material gave way in effectiveness to the broadcast and to the loud speaker." (page 81) What Innis has failed to do in this part of his essay is to make a structural analysis of the modalities of the visual and the audible. He is merely assuming that an extension of information in space has a centralizing power regardless of the human faculty that is amplified and extended. But whereas the visual power extended by print does indeed extend the power to organize a spatial continuum, the auditory power extended electrically does in effect abolish space and time alike. Visual technology creates a centre-margin pattern of organization whether by literacy or by industry and a price system. But electric technology is instant and omnipresent and creates multiple centres-without-margins. Visual technology whether by literacy or by industry creates nations as spatially uniform and homogeneous and connected. But electric technology creates not the nation but the tribe — not the superficial association of equals but the cohesive depth pattern of the totally involved kinship groups. Visual technologies, whether based on papyrus or paper, foster fragmentation and specialism, armies and empires. Electric technology favours not the fragmentary but the integral; not the mechanical but the organic. It had not occurred to Innis that electricity is in effect an extension of the nervous system as a kind of global membrane. As an economic historian he had such a rich experience of the technological extensions of the bodily powers that it is not surprising that he failed to note the character of this most recent and surprising of human extensions.

There is one department in which Innis never fails, and in which the flavour of Innisence is never lacking — his humour. Humour is of the essence of his aphoristic association of incongruities. His technique of discovery by the juxtaposition of forms lends itself everywhere to a series of dramatic surprises. On page 77 in the midst of considering the revolt of the American colonies and nineteenth-century wars he suddenly observes a parallel with the press wars of Hearst and Pulitzer as related to the emergence of the comic strip. He is unrivalled in his power to discover choice items in contemporary history to illuminate grave matters of archaeology. Referring to the neglect of the horse as a factor in military history, he recalls that "E. J. Dillon remarked concerning a mounted policeman that he was always surprised by the look of intelligence on the horse's face." (page 95) The mosaic structure of insights employed in the work of the later Innis is never far removed from the comic irony of an Abraham Lincoln. Innis found that his technique of insight engendered a perpetual entertainment of surprises and of intellectual comedy.

To record the intellectual influences that shaped the work of Innis would be a large, if rewarding, task. His studies at the University of Chicago after the first war occurred at a most favorable time. The work of Emile Durkheim, Max Weber and John Dewey had fecundated a new group of economic and social studies that flowered in the writings of Thorsten Veblen, John Dewey, George Herbert Mead and Robert Ezra Park. These men created an atmosphere at Chicago in the 1920s that attracted and inspired many able students. Most of these men had, like Innis, spent their youth in small towns. The speedy growth of the metropolis after the first war presented an inexhaustible subject for these sociologists, and much of their work was directed to urban study and analysis, using the small town as a basis for comparison and contrast. Innis tended to follow another pattern, though, as we shall see, he was deeply in debt to Robert Ezra Park. Durkheim, the late-nineteenth-century founder of analytic sociology dealt with whole populations. The Chicago school dealt with local communities. Innis is European rather than American in his choice of the larger themes. From Park, however, he learned how to identify the control mechanisms by which a heterogeneous community yet manages to arrange its affairs with some degree of uniformity. Perhaps Innis was aided in this choice by his familiarity with the staple economy of Canada. A semi-industrialized country, rich in major resources like wheat, lumber, minerals, fur, fish, and wood pulp has a peculiar economic and social life compared to a more diversified and developed economy. Innis seized the opportunity to deal with this unique pattern of a staple economy and was not led to follow the popular pattern of urban studies that was being pursued by the exciting and productive Chicago group. I suggest that Innis made the further transition from the history of staples to the history of the media of communication quite naturally. Media are major resources like economic staples. In fact, without railways, the staples of wheat and lumber can scarcely be said to exist. Without the press and the magazine, wood pulp doesn't exist as a staple. In May, 1940, the *Canadian Journal of Economics and Political Science* published an article by Robert Park entitled "Physics and Society." (Reprinted in *Society* by Robert E. Park, Glencoe, Illinois: The Free Press, 1955, pages 301-321.) Park began by citing Walter Bagehot to the effect that society is a social organism maintained by a social process. The theme of his essay is recapitulated this way: "I have gone into some detail in my description of the role and function of communication because it is so obviously fundamental to the social process, and because extensions and improvements which the physical sciences have made to the means of communications are so vital to the existence of society and particularly to that more rationally organized form of society we call civilization." (*Society*, page 314)

The ideas of Park seem to have appealed more to the mind of Harold Innis than to that of any other student of Robert Park. Anybody can hear the Innis note in such observations by Park as the following: "Technological devices have naturally changed men's habits and in doing so, they have necessarily modified the structure and functions of society." (page 308) Again: "From this point of view it seems that every technical device, from the wheelbarrow to the airplane, in so far as it provided a new and more effective means of locomotion, has, or should have, marked an epoch in society. This is so far true as most other important changes in the means of transportation and communication. It is said likewise that every civilization carries in itself the seeds of its own destruction. Such seeds are likely to be the technical devices that introduce a new social order and usher out an old." (*Society*, pages 309-310) In the same year as his "Physics and Society" article, Park published "News as a Form of Knowledge": "I have indicated the role which news plays in the world of politics in so far as it provides the basis for the discussions in which public opinion is formed. The news plays quite as important a role in the world of economic relations, since the price of commodities, including money and securities, as registered in the world market and in every local market dependent upon it, is based on the news." (page 86)

These ideas were not lost on Harold Innis. Indeed, Innis developed them much further than Park did, and should be considered as the most eminent of the Chicago group headed by Robert Park.

Marshall McLuhan's Introduction to Harold Innis' The Bias of Communication
Marshall McLuhan - Unbound (08)

ISBN: 1-58423-051-7
Library of Congress Control Number 2005927213

Marshall McLuhan Unbound Project Editors
Eric McLuhan, W. Terrence Gordon

Published in United States in October 2005 by
Gingko Press, Inc.
5768 Paradise Drive, Suite J · Corte Madera, CA 94925
(415) 924-9615 · Fax (415) 924-9608
email: books@gingkopress.com
http://www.gingkopress.com

Introduced by W. Terrence Gordon

Design, packaging and production: Die Gestalten Verlag, Berlin
Layout and Typography: onlab, Berlin
Fonts: *Dolly* by Underware, *Bullet* by House Industries
Production: Martin Bretschneider, Vinzenz Geppert
Art direction: Robert Klanten

Made in Germany